Chè Lektè,

Se yon plezi pou nou pou pote pou ou bèl ti liv s[...] yon pati nan pwogram nou pou timoun kap debite.

kiryozite syantifik komanse lakay timoun. Kontak ak bèt ak kote bèt yo ap viv-nan lanati oubyen nan yon liv-li souvan nan rasin enterè yon timoun nan sa ki gen rapò avèk lasyans. Te gen yon jèn ti fi yo te rele Jane Goodall ki te renmen obsève lanati bò lakay li anpil. Pasyon sa a te fè li fè premye rechèch li sou makak. Charles Turner, pyonye nan mounn ki espesyalize nan zafè ensèk, te pase anpil tan ap li sou foumi ak lòt ensèk nan liv papa'l yo. Rachel Carson byolojis lanmè, otè epi konsèvasyonis te komanse ekri istwa sou ekirèy lè li te gen uit tan. Se pou nou pwovoke kiryosite kay timoun yo epi wap wè yo menm kap devlope yon anvi pou yo aprann pandan tout vi yo.

Tout bèl parol ak enfomasyon sa yo aprann timoun yo konnen bèl vi ki genyen nan monn bèt la, e anplis aprann konnen pwòp tèt pa yo. Yo ankouraje timoun yo pou fè koneksyon toutbon ak monn nan ki ka ogmante entelijans yo epi fè yo pi byen debite nan lasyans, teknoloji ak matematik (STEM). Lè nou fè lekti sa yo ansanm ak timoun yo, li entèrese yo panse ak tout espès sa yo sou jan yo grandi, sa yo bezwen pou viv ak jan kote yap viv la ye-kit se lè yo sèl, nan bann oubyen nan fanmi.

Plis ke yon senp entwodiksyon syantifik, istwa sou zannimo sa yo fèw konprann e fèw wè bèl lanmou ki genyen nan klas mamifè a. Lè nou montre timounn yo atachman sa a ki genyen nan monn natirèl la, sa ogmante konpreyansyon, jantiyes ak konpasyon nan fason yap konpòte yo ni ak mounn ni ak bèt.

Liv sa a se yon bon chwa pou lakay, bibliyotèk oubyen pou lekòl paske li gen bagay ki ka pwovoke oubyen soutni kiryozite byen bonè lakay nenpòt timoun.

Li liv sa a ak plezi!

Dia

Dia L. Michels
Editè, Platypus Media

Anplis: Nap jwenn lòt materyèl pou ede jèn yo ki renmen fè lekti pou ogmante konesans yo nan sit entènèt sa-a gratis: PlatypusMedia.com.

This book was underwritten by Health and Education for Haiti, LLC, which works collaboratively with the Haitian people to address critical needs, especially in the areas of health and education. For more information, visit HEHOnline.org.

Sante ak Edikasyon pou Ayiti, LLC, se yon òganizasyon ki travay an kolaborasyon ak pèp Ayisyen pou adrese bezwen kritik yo, sitou nan domèn sante ak edikasyon e se òganizasyon sa a ki te sipòte liv sa a. Pou plis enfòmasyon, vizite HEHOnline.org

Cuddled and Carried

Karese'm epi pote'm

Se Dia L. Michels ki ekri liv sa a
epi Mike Speiser ilistre'l

Platypus Media
Washington, D.C., U.S.

My mama grooms me

Manman'm pwòpte'm

and guides me.

epi li gide'm.

My mama cuddles me

Manman'm karese'm

and carries me.

epi li pote'm.

My mama snuggles me

Manman'm pran swen'm

and shelters me.

epi li pwoteje'm.

My mama nurtures me

Manman'm leve'm

and nuzzles me.

epi li edike'm.

My mama nourishes me.

Manman'm banm manje.

My family loves me very much.

Fanmi'm renmenm anpil.

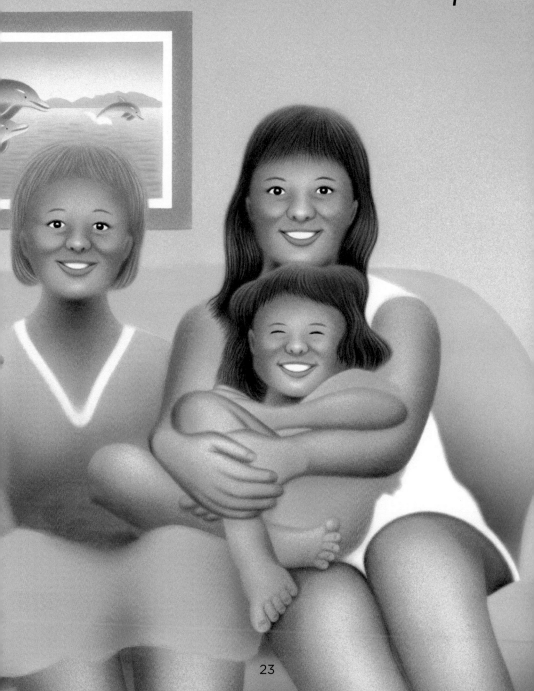

Cuddled and Carried • Karese'm epi pote'm
ISBN 13: 978-1-930775-82-4 | First Edition • March 2020
          Second Edition • July 2023
eBook ISBN 13: 978-1-930775-78-7 | First Edition • March 2020

Written by Dia L. Michels, Text © 2020
Illustrated by Mike Speiser, Illustration © 2020

Part of the Platypus Media collection, Beginnings
Beginnings logo by Hannah Thelen, © 2018 Platypus Media

Haitian Creole Project Manager: Dr. Frank J. Nice, Derwood, MD
Translated by Jean Louijuin Honorè, Jeremie, Grand'Anse, Haiti and
          Pierre Alix Occide, Latibolière, Grand'Anse, Haiti
English Project Manager: Anna Cohen, Washington, D.C.
Cover and Book Design: Hannah Thelen, Platypus Media, Silver Spring, MD
          Holly Harper, Blue Bike Communications, Washington, D.C., and
          Linsey Silver, Element 47 Design, Washington, D.C.

Translated from the English/Spanish book:
          Cuddled and Carried • Consentido y cargado (Stroller-bag edition)
          Paperback ISBN 13: 978-1-93-077565-7 | First Edition • October 2019
          eBook ISBN 13: 978-1-930775-66-4 | First Edition • October 2019

Teacher's Guide available in English at the Educational Resources page of PlatypusMedia.com

Published by: Platypus Media, LLC
          725 8th Street, SE
          Washington, DC 20003
          1-202-546-1674 | Toll-free: 1-877-PLATYPS (1-877-725-8977)
          Info@PlatypusMedia.com | www.PlatypusMedia.com

Distributed to the book trade by: National Book Network
          1-301-459-3366 | Toll-free: 1-800-787-6859
          CustServ@nbnbooks.com | www.NBNbooks.com

Library of Congress Control Number: 2019052798

11 10 9 8 7 6 5 4 3 2

Printed in the United States

Ekip pwojè

Dia L. Michels se yon editè entènasyonal ki genyen prim nan lasyans e ki ekri liv sou jan paran dwe fè levasyon timoun epi ki angaje'l pou fè pwomosyon pou atachman paran ak pitit. Li ekri plis ke yon douzèn liv pou timoun ak granmoun. Nou ka jwenn li nan adrès sa a: Dia@PlatypusMedia.com.

Travay atistik Mike Speiser te parèt sou po liv pitit bèt sovaj yo ak nan mize atistik yo rele Leigh Yawkey Woodson. Li angaje'l nan travay pou pwoteje monn natirèl la pou jenerasyon kap vini yo. Nou ka jwenn li nan adrès sa a: Mike@PlatypusMedia.com.

Dr. Frank J. Nice gen plis pase karant ane depi li ap travay kòm konsiltan, konferansye epi ekri liv sou medikaman ak alètman. Dr. Nice se yon manm fondatè òganizasyon ki rele Sante ak Edikasyon pou Ayiti ki se ki ede ayisyen bati legliz ak òfelina e ki pèmèt elèv yo konn ayiti ak monn nan pi byen, ede ayisyen pran swen legliz yo ak dirije sant sante yo. Li renmen montre ak aprann anpil bagay ak zanmi ayisyen li yo sitou zanmi elèv li yo.

Mèt Honoré Jean Louijuin se yon tradiktè epi entèprèt anpil misyon medikal ak tout lòt misyon, epi pwofesè anglè depi plis pase disèt lane. Li se fondatè ak direktè lekòl Anglè "Light Institute" ki gen onz lane depi li te ouvri 'l nan Leon ak Jeremi, Haiti. Depi lane 2008 lap kowòdone diferan pwojè kòm volontè pou pawas Sen Franswa Dasiz ozetazini nan pawas Sen Pòl nan Leyon, Jeremi, Ayiti ki se Pawas Sè Pawas sa a e li se moun zòn nan. Nou ka jwenn Mèt Honoré Jean Louijuin nan adrès sa a: honoloui@yahoo.fr.

Pierre Alix Occide te fè vennsèt lane ap viv Ozetazini avan li te retounen vinn viv an ayiti nan lane 2007. Li gen yon lisans nan Jesyon nan inivèsite Denver Etazini. Konnye a li ap travay kòm pwofesè Anglè, tradiktè e entèprèt pou anpil misyon medikal ak lòt. Li angaje'l nan fondasyon jèn yo nan latibolyè, Grandans, Ayiti ki se lakay li e lap travay pou yon pi bon edikasyon pou tout jèn an ayiti. Ou ka jwenn li sou WhatsApp nan nimewo sa a (509)39933974.

What Do We Call Them?

Kouvèti	Animal Name *Non bèt yo*	
	English • *Anglè*	Creole • *Kreyol*
Kouvèti	Bobcat	Gwo chat
p. 2-3	Goose	Zwa
p. 4	Panda	Panda
p. 5	Wolf	Lou
p. 6	Manatee	Manati
p. 7	Dolphin	Dofen
p. 8	Orangutan	Oranoutan
p. 9	Koala	Koala
p. 10-11	Sea Otter	Lout
p. 12	Elephant	Elefan
p. 13	Seal	Fòk
p. 14-15	Snow Leopard	Leopa nèj
p. 16	Penguin	Pengwen
p. 17	Flamingo	Flanman (Zwazo)
p. 18-19	Fox	Rena
p. 20	Polar Bear	Gwo Lous
p. 21-23	Human	Moun
p. 25	Cougar	Pouma

Kijan nou rele yo?

Baby Animal Name *Non pitit bèt yo*		Group Name *Non gwoup bèt yo*	
English • *Anglè*	Creole • *Kreyol*	English • *Anglè*	Creole • *Kreyol*
Cub	Ti chat	Clowder/Clutter/Pounce	Gwoup
Gosling	Ti zwa	Gaggle	Bann
Cub	Ti panda	Group	Gwoup
Pup	Ti lou	Pack	Pakèt
Calf	Ti manati	Aggregation/Herd	Twoupo
Calf	Ti dofen	Pod	Bann
Baby/Infant	Bebe	Troup/Buffoonery	Gwoup
Joey	Ti koala	Population/Colony	Popilasyon
Pup	Ti lout	Raft	Pakèt
Calf	Ti elefan	Herd	Twoupo
Pup	Ti fòk	Pod	Bann
Cub	Ti leopa nèj	Leap	Gwoup
Chick	Ti pengwen	Colony	Kolonn
Chick	Ti flanman	Flamboyance/Stand	Bann
Cub	Ti rena	Skulk	Gwoup
Cub	Ti lous	Celebration	Kolonn
Baby	Bebe	Community	Kominote
Cub	Ti pouma	Pack/Pride	Pakèt

Animal Classes
Klas bèt yo

ACTIVITY: Using these definitions, match each animal pictured in the book to its correct class. Which classes appear more than once? Which do not appear at all?

AKTIVITE: Itilize definisyon sa yo, mete chak bèt ki nan liv sa a nan klas pa'l. Ki klas ki parèt plis pase yon fwa e kiyès ki pa parèt ditou?

Bird / *Zwazo*

An animal that has wings and is covered with feathers.

Ex. eagles, robins, flamingos

Se yon bèt ki gen zèl epi kò li kouvri ak plim.

Ex: èg, wouj gòj, flanman

Reptile / *Reptil*

An animal that is cold blooded, lays eggs, and has a body covered with scales or hard parts.

Ex. turtles, crocodiles, snakes

Se yon bèt ki gen san frèt ,ki ponn ze epi ki gen yon kò ki plen kal oubyen ki gen po rèd.

Ex: tòti, krokodil, koulèv

Fish / *Pwason*

An animal that lives in water and has gills and fins on their body.

Ex. goldfish, carp, sharks

Se yon bèt ki viv nan dlo e ki gen zèl ak zòrèy nan kò yo.

Ex: pwason wouj, kap, rekin

Mammal / *Mamifè*

An animal that has hair/fur, is endothermic, has a backbone, and feeds milk to its young.

Ex. horses, dogs, humans

Se yon bèt ki gen cheve/pwal, ki abitye ak chalè, ki gen yon gwo zo nan do'l epi ki bay pitit li tete.

Ex: cheval, chen, moun

Amphibian / *Anfibi*

An animal that can live both on land and in water. When they are first born, they have an aquatic gill-breathing larval stage before typically developing into a lung-breathing adult.

ex. frogs, toads, salamanders

Se yon bèt ki ka viv sou latè tankou nan dlo. Lè yo fenk fèt se nan zòrèy yo pran souf nan dlo epi zòrèy la vinn tounen poumon lè yo vinn gran.

Ex: krapo, gounouy, salamann

Arthropod / *Atwopòd*

An animal that has more than four jointed legs.

Ex. bees, spiders, crabs

Se yon bèt ki gen plis pase kat janm (Bèt kò yo divise an plizyè pati).

Ex: abèy, zarenyen, krab

Answers

Repons

Mammal Class / Klas bèt yo:
bobcat/gwo chat, panda/panda, wolf/lou, manatee/manati, dolphin/dofen, orangutan/oranoutan, koala/koala, sea otter/lout, elephant/elefan, seal/fòk, snow leopard/leopa nèj, fox/rena, polar bear/gwo lous, human/moun, cougar/pouma

Bird Class / Klas zwazo yo:
goose/zwa, penguin/pengwen, flamingo/flanman

29

Care and Attachment
Swen ak atachman

Mothers care for their babies in many ways. Each animal baby has different needs based on their habitat, how fast they grow, and the social behavior of their species. Scientists identify four categories of care for mammals.

ACTIVITY: Review the definitions provided here and try to match the mammals in this book to the way the mother cares for her babies.

Manman pran swen pitit anpil fason. Chak ti bèt gen bezwen ki diferan de yon lòt selon kote yap viv la ,jan yo grandi e ki espès yo ye. Mounn ki pratike lasyans idantifye kat kategori swen lakay mamifè yo.

AKTIVITE: Gade definisyon yo ba ou la a epi eseye konpare mamifè yo nan liv sa a ak jan manman pran swen pitit yo .

Cache / *Kache*

Ex. deer, rabbits / *Ex: sèf, lapin*

HINT: There are no cache mammals in this book.

ENDIKASYON: Nan liv sa a pa genyen mamifè kache.

Follow / *Swiv*

Ex. giraffes, cows / *Ex: jiraf, bèf*

HINT: Look for babies that walk or swim by mom.

ENDIKASYON: Chache ti bèt ke se manman yo ki montre yo mache ak naje.

Nest / *Nich*

Ex. dogs, cats / *Ex: chen, chat*

HINT: Look for animals snuggling together.

ENDIKASYON: Chache bèt ke youn toujou ap chofe lòt.

Carry / *Pote*

Ex. kangaroos, humans /
Ex. kangourou, moun

HINT: Look for babies that are often held, or hold onto mom.

ENDIKASYON: Chache pitit ke se manman yo ki souvan pote yo ak kenbe yo.

Cache Mammals / *Mamifè ki kache*

These animals are mature at birth. Mothers hide their babies in a safe place, returning every twelve hours or so. Their milk is high in protein and fat to sustain the babies for a long time between feedings.

Bèt sa yo fèt ak tout matirite yo. Manman yo sere pitit yo yon kote ki an sekirite. Yo retounen chak douzèdtan ou menm plis ke sa pou bay yo tete paske lèt yo gen anpil pwoteyin ak grès ki ka kenbe yo pou anpil tan.

Follow Mammals / *Mamifè ki swiv*

These mammals are also mature at birth, but follow their mothers wherever they go. Since the baby is always near the mother and feeds often, the mother's milk is relatively low in protein and fat.

Mamifè sa yo fèt ak tout matirite yo tou, men yo swiv manman yo tout kote yo fè. Akòz pitit sa yo toujou bò kote manman yo, yo tete souvan paske lèt manman yo pa gen anpil pwoteyin ak grès.

Nest Mammals / *Mamifè ki fè nich*

These animals are relatively immature at birth. They need the nest and closeness of their siblings for warmth. They nurse several times a day. The mother's milk has less protein and fat than cache mammals, but more than follow mammals.

Bèt sa yo pa genyen matirite lè yo fenk fèt. Yo bezwen nich yo e yo toujou kole ansanm pou yo ka chofe. Yo tete plizyè fwa nan yon jounen. Lèt manman yo gen pi piti pwoteyin ak grès ke mamifè kache yo, men yo gen plis pase mamifè swiv yo.

Carry Mammals / *Mamifè yo pote*

These animals are the most immature at birth, need the warmth of the mother's body, are carried constantly, and feed around the clock. The mother's milk has low levels of fat and protein.

Bèt sa yo se yo menm ki plis pa gen matirite lè yo fenk fèt. Yo bezwen chalè kò manman yo ki pote yo tout tan epi yo tete tout lajounen. Lèt manman yo pa gen anpil grès ak pwoteyin.

U.S.-China Relations After Resolution of Taiwan's Status

Roger Cliff, David A. Shlapak

Prepared for the United States Air Force

PROJECT AIR FORCE

The research described in this report was sponsored by the United States Air Force under Contracts F49642-01-C-0003 and FA7014-06-C-0001. Further information may be obtained from the Strategic Planning Division, Directorate of Plans, Hq USAF.

Library of Congress Cataloging-in-Publication Data

Cliff, Roger
     U.S.–China relations after resolution of Taiwan's status / Roger Cliff,
David A. Shlapak.
        p. cm.
     Includes bibliographical references.
     ISBN 978-0-8330-4036-7 (pbk. : alk. paper)
     1. National security—Taiwan. 2. China—Military policy—21st century.
3. United States—Military policy—21st century. 4. Taiwan—Foreign relations—
China. 5. China—Foreign relations—Taiwan. 6. United States—Foreign relations—
China. 7. China—Foreign relations—United States. 8. United States—Foreign
relations—Taiwan. 9. Taiwan—Foreign relations—United States. I. Shlapak,
David A. II. Title.

UA853.T28C55 2007
327.73051—dc22

2007010344

The RAND Corporation is a nonprofit research organization providing objective analysis and effective solutions that address the challenges facing the public and private sectors around the world. RAND's publications do not necessarily reflect the opinions of its research clients and sponsors.

RAND® is a registered trademark.

Cover photo: 060906-N-9643K-006 Pearl Harbor, Hawaii (Sept. 6, 2006) - Chinese Sailors man the rails aboard the destroyer Qingdao (DDG 113) as they arrive in Pearl Harbor. Two ships representing China's Navy, the destroyer Qingdao and the oiler Hongzehu (AOR 881) arrived in Pearl Harbor for a routine port visit. U.S. Navy photo by Mass Communication Specialist Joe Kane (RELEASED)

Published 2007 by the RAND Corporation
1776 Main Street, P.O. Box 2138, Santa Monica, CA 90407-2138
1200 South Hayes Street, Arlington, VA 22202-5050
4570 Fifth Avenue, Suite 600, Pittsburgh, PA 15213-2665
RAND URL: http://www.rand.org/
To order RAND documents or to obtain additional information, contact
Distribution Services: Telephone: (310) 451-7002;
Fax: (310) 451-6915; Email: order@rand.org

Preface

This monograph was motivated by an effort to assess the nature of U.S.-China relations after the resolution of Taiwan's status. It stems from the recognition that the nature and extent of the effects on Sino-U.S. ties of an end to the cross-strait standoff will be strongly conditioned by *what* that resolution is and *how* it came about.

This document identifies the principal pathways by which Taiwan's status might be resolved and analyzes the likely consequences for U.S.-China relations. It is intended to be of use to policymakers, military planners, and policy researchers concerned about the future of U.S.-China relations and its implications for U.S. military planning.

The research reported here was sponsored by the Assistant Deputy Chief of Staff for Long-Range Planning, Headquarters, U.S. Air Force (AF/XPX). The work was conducted as part of a fiscal year 2005 project, "The U.S.-China Security Relationship: Taiwan and Beyond," within the Strategy and Doctrine Program of RAND Project AIR FORCE. It is part of an ongoing Project AIR FORCE effort to assess the nature and implications of the growth in Chinese military power. Previous publications from this effort include

- Roger Cliff, Mark Burles, Michael S. Chase, Derek Eaton, Kevin L. Pollpeter, *Entering the Dragon's Lair: Chinese Antiaccess Strategies and Their Implications for the United States*, MG-524-AF, 2007.
- Evan S. Medeiros, Roger Cliff, Keith Crane, and James C. Mulvenon, *A New Direction for China's Defense Industry*, MG-334-AF, 2005.

- Keith Crane, Roger Cliff, Evan Medeiros, James C. Mulvenon, and William Overholt, *Modernizing China's Military: Opportunities and Constraints*, MG-260-1-AF, 2005.
- Kevin Pollpeter, *U.S.-China Security Management: Assessing the Military-to-Military Relationship*, MG-143-AF, 2004.
- Zalmay Khalilzad, David T. Orletsky, Jonathan Pollack, Kevin Pollpeter, Angel M. Rabasa, David A. Shlapak, Abram N. Shulsky, Ashley J. Tellis, *The United States and Asia: Toward a New U.S. Strategy and Force Posture*, MR-1315-AF, 2001.
- Roger Cliff, *The Military Potential of China's Commercial Technology*, MR-1292-AF, 2001.
- Erica Strecker Downs, *China's Quest for Energy Security*, MR-1244-AF, 2000.
- Richard Sokolsky, Angel Rabasa, and C. R. Neu, *The Role of Southeast Asia in U.S. Strategy Toward China*, MR-1170-AF, 2000.
- Abram N. Shulsky, *Deterrence Theory and Chinese Behavior*, MR-1161-AF, 2000.
- Mark Burles and Abram N. Shulsky, *Patterns in China's Use of Force: Evidence from History and Doctrinal Writings*, MR-1160-AF, 2000.
- Michael D. Swaine and Ashley J. Tellis, *Interpreting China's Grand Strategy: Past, Present, and Future*, MR-1121-AF, 2000.
- Daniel L. Byman and Roger Cliff, *China's Arms Sales: Motivations and Implications*, MR-1119-AF, 1999.
- Zalmay Khalilzad, Abram N. Shulsky, Daniel Byman, Roger Cliff, David T. Orletsky, David A. Shlapak, and Ashley J. Tellis, *The United States and a Rising China: Strategic and Military Implications*, MR-1082-AF, 1999.
- Mark Burles, *Chinese Policy Toward Russia and the Central Asian Republics*, MR-1045-AF, 1999.

The information in this monograph is current as of September 2006.

RAND Project AIR FORCE

RAND Project AIR FORCE (PAF), a division of the RAND Corporation, is the U.S. Air Force's federally funded research and development center for studies and analyses. PAF provides the Air Force with independent analyses of policy alternatives affecting the development, employment, combat readiness, and support of current and future aerospace forces. Research is conducted in four programs: Aerospace Force Development; Manpower, Personnel, and Training; Resource Management; and Strategy and Doctrine.

Additional information about PAF is available on our Web site at http://www.rand.org/paf.

Contents

Figure and Tables

Summary

Although it appears unlikely that the question of Taiwan's status and ultimate relationship to China will be resolved any time soon, it is instructive to speculate about how its resolution might affect U.S.-China relations. There are, broadly speaking, ten different logical possibilities for trajectories that the cross-Strait relationship could follow. Four of them are peaceful (see pp. 6–11):

- continuation of the current unresolved status quo
- peaceful unification
- peaceful independence
- a compromise resolution.

Six involve Chinese use of force against Taiwan (see pp. 11–19):

- violent unification with U.S. intervention
- violent unification without U.S. intervention
- violent independence with U.S. intervention
- violent independence without U.S. intervention
- violent irresolution with U.S. intervention
- violent irresolution without U.S. intervention.

Looking across all these cases reveals that simply assuming that the Taiwan situation has been "resolved" is hardly enough to understand the nature of the subsequent security relationship between China and the United States. Instead, the manner and mode in which the Taiwan question is decided will make a great deal of difference. To the

extent one can generalize, the obvious appears to be true: The consequences of peaceful outcomes—including continued peaceful irresolution—are both more predictable and generally better for relations between Washington and Beijing (see pp. 6–11, 20–22).

In contrast, nonpeaceful resolutions of Taiwan's status could cause U.S.-China relations to fall anywhere from reasonable amity to a Cold War–like confrontation, depending on the circumstances surrounding the conflict and its outcome. If the result is formal independence for Taiwan, subsequent U.S-China relations will likely be cooperative. If the result is forcible unification for Taiwan, the United States and China will likely find themselves in a hostile cold war (see pp. 11–18, 20–22).

For more than 25 years, U.S. policy has, above all else, sought to ensure that any resolution of Taiwan's status occurs peacefully. The implication of the findings of this study is that, as China's power and confidence in its military capabilities grow and therefore the possibility of Beijing attempting to bring about unification through force increases, preventing such an attempt from occurring while maintaining the capability to defeat it will become increasingly important even as it becomes increasingly difficult.

Acknowledgements

The authors are grateful to the other members of our project team, Steve Brock, Michael Chase, John Fei, Nina Hachigian, Michael Lostumbo, Evan Medeiros, William Overholt, Toy Reid, Scot Tanner, and Eric Valko, for their suggestions and insights. They are also grateful to Eric Heginbotham of RAND and Richard Bush of the Brookings Institution for thoughtful and incisive reviews, to Andrew Hoehn and Cynthia Cook of Project AIR FORCE for their support and patience, to Sarah Harting for compiling the bibliography and ensuring that the document is properly formatted, and to Phyllis Gilmore for editing it so that our points are communicated clearly. The authors take sole responsibility for any errors or shortcomings in this report.

CHAPTER ONE

Near-Term Prospects

At present, the most obvious and likely source of conflict between the United States and China is Taiwan. This has prompted many to wonder what might cause conflict between the United States and China if Taiwan's current uncertain status were to be resolved. Resolution of Taiwan's status, however, would not necessarily eliminate the possibility of tension or even conflict between Washington and Beijing. Indeed, perhaps the dominant determinant of the likelihood of conflict between the United States and China after resolution of Taiwan's status would be precisely *how* that status was resolved. It is useful, therefore, to examine the ways in which Taiwan's status could be resolved and how the events surrounding that resolution would likely shape the subsequent U.S.-China relationship.

In making this examination, it is worth noting at the start that Taiwan's status is unlikely to be decided any time soon. On the one hand, no Chinese Communist Party (CCP) leadership is likely to risk allowing Taiwan to peaceably formalize its independence. The CCP has to a large extent based its legitimacy on restoring China to "its rightful place in the world" and on reversing the effects of China's "century of humiliation" (from the first Opium War of 1839 to the founding of the People's Republic in 1949). However peripheral Taiwan originally was to the integrity of the Chinese nation, it has now become a potent symbol of China's subjugation at the hands of the imperial powers.[1]

---

[1] Reportedly, when the Empress Dowager Cixi, China's effective ruler at the time of China's defeat in the Sino-Japanese War of 1894–1895, was told that Japan's terms of victory included the ceding of Taiwan, she had to be told what "Taiwan" was.

Only by recovering Taiwan can the nation again be made whole and the humiliations of the past be erased. Any leadership group that allowed Taiwan to become formally independent would be at risk of losing its legitimacy both within the CCP and in the eyes of the Chinese public.[2] Mao Zedong's personal power and prestige were such that he could ignore the Taiwan issue without risking his hold on power, but no current or future Chinese leader or group of leaders is likely to have that luxury.[3] This will be particularly true over the next few years, as president Hu Jintao and premier Wen Jiabao work to complete the consolidation of their power in the post-Jiang Zemin era.

Similarly, Taiwan is unlikely to peacefully accept any form of unification in the near future. It will certainly not happen under the current Chen Shui-bian administration, since his party aspires to full independence for Taiwan. Even if Chen's successor, to be elected in 2008, is from one of the parties that nominally aspires to eventual unification between Taiwan and mainland China, and those parties retain their current control of Taiwan's legislature, it is implausible that there would be enough domestic support for unification for the government to feel that it could legitimately take such a dramatic step—even if it wanted to. Currently, opinion surveys consistently indicate that only about two percent of Taiwan's population favor immediate unification with China, while more than 20 percent hope that Taiwan will eventually become a fully independent state.[4] By and large, the Taiwan body

---

[2]   Cliff (1996). Although China remains a one-party dictatorship, as the Chinese social and political system continues to open up, public opinion is acquiring increasing influence in Chinese politics, including policy toward Taiwan. Interviews with mainland Chinese Taiwan specialists held in China during February and March 2006 reinforced this point.

[3]   It is possible, however, that Beijing and Taipei could reach some form of mutual accommodation that would allow the final resolution of the Taiwan issue to be deferred until some future time. See the "Compromise Resolution" section in Chapter Two.

[4]   Mainland Affairs Council, 2006. When polled, about 60 percent of Taiwan's adult population consistently indicate either that they want the status quo to continue indefinitely or that they are undecided about whether they want Taiwan to eventually unify with the mainland or become independent. Chen is widely believed to want independence for Taiwan and was reelected in 2004 with more than 50 percent of the vote, so it is possible that support for Taiwan independence is actually significantly higher than the 20 to 25 percent indicated by polls. The low percentage of Taiwan's population in favor of immediate unification, on

politic appears to have a strong preference for the status quo, however strategically uncomfortable that may be for leaders in Washington, Beijing, and Taipei.

There also seems to be little chance of Taiwan's status being resolved violently in the near term. If China were to attempt to seize or bully Taiwan into unification through the use of military force, the United States retains the ability to intervene and likely prevent the People's Republic of China (PRC) from succeeding.[5] At the very least, the possibility of U.S. intervention almost certainly constitutes a powerful deterrent to any possible Chinese adventurism.

While Beijing has little hope of achieving unification through force in the near term, Taiwan has similarly little chance of achieving independence as a result of a conflict with the mainland. Even if a Chinese use of force against Taiwan were unsuccessful, and even if Taiwan gained widespread recognition as an independent nation, this would probably not constitute final resolution of Taiwan's status; the PRC would likely refuse to acknowledge or accept Taiwan's independence. Instead, Taiwan's independence would probably be regarded in China as a temporary situation that would be reversed as soon as China had the military capability to do so.

For all these reasons, for at least the next four or five years, the most likely possibility with regard to Taiwan's status is that *the current unresolved but peaceful situation will continue unchanged.* If there were a military conflict in the Taiwan Strait in this time frame, there is a small chance that China would prevail decisively, leaving the United States and its partners (if any) to decide whether to try to "liberate"

---

the other hand, may in part be a consequence of Beijing's proposed "One Country, Two Systems" formula for unification, under which Taiwan would have to accept a status subordinate to Beijing. The current leadership in Beijing has so far shown little sign of flexibility on this issue; even if they did, it seems unlikely that such a shift would suffice to produce a majority of Taiwan's population favoring immediate unification.

[5] It is possible that the United States could perceive that Taiwan had provoked the PRC attack and consequently refrain from intervening. In this case, it is possible that China could succeed in unifying with Taiwan through force in the near term. It seems unlikely, however, that Taipei would be so imprudent as to take actions that the United States could perceive as unambiguously provocative.

Taiwan. The more likely outcome, however—assuming U.S. intervention—would be a Chinese defeat, leaving Beijing licking its wounds but refusing to accept the definitive loss of Taiwan.

For Taiwan's status to be resolved, one or more of the following will probably have to change: (1) the nature of the regime in Beijing, (2) the military balance in the Taiwan Strait, or (3) the U.S. security commitment to Taiwan. Such changes are only likely to occur over the longer term (more than five years). Moreover, even if one or more of those developments occurs, it is possible that Taiwan's status will remain unresolved. Combined with the two primary possibilities (peaceful irresolution or violent irresolution) that prevail in the near term, there are a total of ten distinct longer-term future situations with regard to Taiwan's status, which will be discussed in Chapter Two of this monograph.

Longer-Term Possibilities

This chapter describes ten logical possibilities for the China-Taiwan situation, which are depicted in tree form in Figure 2.1. As shown, six of the possibilities involve violence, and four—including the continuation of the current peaceful status quo—do not. Of the cases that turn violent,

Figure 2.1
Ten Possible Outcomes Between China and Taiwan

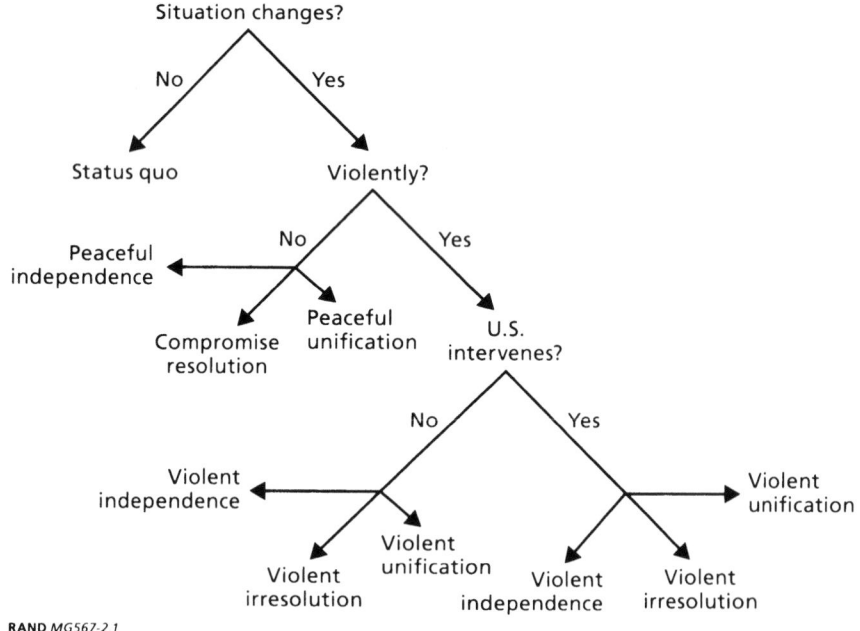

RAND *MG567-2.1*

the United States chooses to engage actively in Taiwan's defense in three and to abstain from involvement in the other three.[1]

Nonviolent Outcomes

Status Quo Continued

In this situation, the current circumstances of an unresolved but peaceful cross-strait conundrum continue indefinitely. China continues to claim Taiwan as part of its territory and implicitly threatens to use force to achieve unification, but does not actually do so. Taiwan neither accepts unification nor declares independence, while the United States maintains its simultaneous commitments to a peaceful resolution of the standoff and to no independence for Taiwan.

If either Beijing or Taipei gave evidence of becoming more flexible about Taiwan's status, it would be possible to reduce cross-strait tensions through stabilization proposals, such as unilateral or negotiated measures for enhancing cooperation and trust and reducing the suspicions of each side that the other might change the status quo unilaterally. For example, if Beijing indicated that it was willing to consider a unification arrangement in which mainland China and Taiwan were equal partners, as opposed to the current "One Country, Two Systems" proposal—which stipulates that Taiwan would be a "special administrative region" under the mainland government—perceptions that Taiwan's status could be resolved peacefully would probably increase, resulting in a concomitant decrease in military tensions. This would also be true if Taipei indicated that it was willing to accept the "one China" principle and concede that Taiwan and mainland China were both parts of a single political and cultural entity, even if the precise nature and contour of that entity was left unspecified. In such a situation, although Taiwan would likely continue to be an important issue in the U.S.-China relationship, it could become significantly less

---

[1] This breakdown should not be interpreted as meaning that there is a 60-percent chance of cross-strait violence or that in the event of war the probability of U.S. intervention is 50 percent. Instead, we are simply laying out the logical possibilities.

prominent than it is to today, and other issues between the two countries, such as trade imbalances, human rights, or the situation on the Korean peninsula, might come to dominate the relationship.[2]

Signs of reduced flexibility about Taiwan's status, on the other hand, would elevate cross-strait tensions. Examples of this would be if Taiwan's proindependence parties were to gain complete control over the political system—by winning a majority in Taiwan's legislature and maintaining their grip on the presidency—or if Beijing were to issue an ultimatum or publish a timeline for Taiwan's unification with the mainland.

As long as Beijing continued to threaten to achieve unification through force, Taiwan refused to accept Bejing's unification offers, and the United States remained committed to Taiwan's defense, however, the possibility of war over Taiwan would likely remain the dominant issue in the U.S.-China security relationship.[3] Moreover, if China's economic growth rate remained high and if its military continued to modernize, the possibility of military conflict would be increasingly alarming from the perspective of the United States and Taiwan.

Peaceful Unification

Although political and social trends in Taiwan appear to be working against prospects for a nonviolent unification with the mainland, the possibility cannot be ruled out. Peaceful unification would most likely first require both the emergence of a consensus on a Taiwan national identity that is at once Chinese and Taiwanese *and* on the emergence of a stable, mature democracy on the mainland comparable to those in Taiwan, Japan, and South Korea today—otherwise, the people of

---

[2] See the section on "Compromise Resolution" (pp. 10–11), for the implications of a situation in which Beijing or Taipei not only proposed a more flexible alternative to its current position but both sides were actually able to agree on one of them.

[3] It is possible, but unlikely, that the United States would withdraw its security commitment to Taiwan. This might occur, for example, if Washington perceived Taiwan's government to be deliberately provoking mainland China into attacking it. The cases in which China actually might attack Taiwan and the United States would not intervene are discussed in the sections that follow.

Taiwan would have little confidence in any promises of autonomy that Beijing might extend.[4]

The emergence of a democratic China would undoubtedly transform the nature of U.S.-China relations. There is an extensive, though not unanimous, body of analysis that suggests that mature democracies rarely, if ever, go to war with each other.[5] There is, however, likewise evidence that states undergoing the transition to democracy can be more war-prone than others.[6] Thus, the relationship between the United States (or Taiwan) and a *democratizing* China could be highly unstable, and any democratic transition in a country the size of China is likely to be the work of many years, if not generations. If this transition period were successfully negotiated, however, and a democracy were to emerge on the mainland that was mature and stable enough for Taiwan to unify with the mainland voluntarily, relations between Washington and Beijing would likely be transformed as well. Although some tensions and suspicions between the two sides would continue, just as between any two countries, the chances of actual conflict between the United States and a democratic China would be much lower than they are today, particularly with the Taiwan issue also resolved.

Peaceful unification could also be effected through some looser form of political relationship, such as a confederacy or commonwealth, in which both Taiwan and the mainland had equal standing and which could be voluntarily dissolved at the initiative of either party. Achieving this type of largely symbolic "unification" would not necessarily require mainland China to become a democracy, and the effect on U.S.-China relations would be similar to that described in the section below called "Compromise Resolutions."

---

[4]   It is, of course, possible that a democratic transition on the mainland would not resolve Taiwan's status. Democracy in China is probably a necessary but certainly not sufficient condition for peaceful unification.

[5]   Brown et al. (1997); Farber and Gowa (1995), pp. 123-146; Spiro (1994), pp. 50–86.

[6]   Mansfield and Snyder (2005).

Peaceful Independence

It is similarly unlikely that Taiwan could peacefully achieve independence—that Beijing would formally recognize and accept it as an independent state—without a fundamental transformation of the Chinese polity. As implied above, having all but officially renounced the pursuit of socialist goals, the Chinese regime has, to a large extent, premised its legitimacy on nationalist objectives: turning China into a rich and powerful modern nation and repairing the injuries China suffered in its period of weakness. Allowing Taiwan to become formally independent would be seen, both inside and outside the CCP, as defaulting on this mission. During negotiations with Britain over the recovery of Hong Kong in the early 1980s, China's supreme leader at the time, Deng Xiaoping, stated that any Chinese government that failed to recover Hong Kong on the expiration of the New Territories lease in 1997 would be forced to step down from power; this would likely be equally true for a CCP government that allowed Taiwan to become independent.

It is possible, however, that a regime other than the CCP, one whose legitimacy was perhaps not so strongly based on the restoration of national unity, could be more flexible on this issue. The most obvious candidate for such a regime would be a mature, stable democracy, which would derive its legitimacy from the will of the people.[7] It is also possible, however, that even a nondemocratic government could find some source other than nationalism on which to base its rule.[8]

Regardless of its form, a Chinese regime that peacefully allowed Taiwan to become independent would almost by definition be both very different from the current leadership and highly pragmatic about how it approached foreign affairs. Competition and conflict with the United States would still be possible, but most likely only when clear U.S. and Chinese interests were involved and when the Chinese gov-

---

[7] A democratic government would not *necessarily* be willing to allow Taiwan to become independent, however. Indeed, strong nationalist sentiment within the population could cause a democratic government to be even more belligerent on the Taiwan issue than the present regime.

[8] Perhaps a modernized form of Confucianism could make a comeback as a supporting ideology. See Robertson and Liu (2006).

ernment expected the material benefits of a clash with the United States to exceed its probable costs. Such conflict would not likely be based on purely ideational constructs, such as what geographic entities China's national territory ought to comprise.

Compromise Resolution

Absent a political transformation in mainland China, the best chance for a peaceful resolution of Taiwan's status probably lies in an arrangement somewhere between formal independence and formal unification, a state that might be called "peaceful in-betweenness." Politicians and analysts in Taiwan and the United States have proposed a number of such formulas. One possibility would be an agreement to leave Taiwan's status unresolved for some period, with Beijing promising not to use force as long as Taiwan refrained from attempting to formalize its independence. Although this outcome would not be a true or final resolution of Taiwan's status, the period in question could be very long or even unlimited, with the two sides agreeing to leave Taiwan's status unresolved until they both come to an agreement on the issue.

The current Chinese regime, including the new "fourth generation" leaders, has so far shown no interest in such schemes, but it is not inconceivable that a future party leadership would be both willing and politically capable of accepting an arrangement with Taiwan if the costs to regime stability of continued cross-strait tensions began to outweigh the value of this specific play of the nationalism card. The successive leaderships of the People's Republic of China have frequently surprised outside observers with their ability to make fundamental changes to core policies. Thus, this is one way in which Taiwan's status could actually be resolved peacefully that might not necessarily imply a fundamental change in the nature of the Chinese regime. As in the case of "Peaceful Independence," however, a Chinese regime that would be willing to accept such an arrangement would almost by definition be one that was more pragmatic in its approach to foreign affairs.[9] Although the possibility for competition and conflict between

---

[9]   The authors are grateful to Richard Bush of the Brookings Institution for this observation.

the United States and such a regime would still exist, the new attitude of the Chinese government, along with the elimination of the Taiwan flashpoint, would significantly reduce the risk of war between the two countries.

Conflict Involving the United States

Violent Irresolution with U.S. Intervention

This situation would occur if China attempted to use force to achieve unification, the United States intervened, and China's efforts were defeated, but Beijing refused to accept Taiwan's independence.[10] Analysis at RAND has found that a conflict between the United States and China over Taiwan would likely be confined to the use of conventional weapons, even though both the United States and China possess nuclear weapons, and that it would not likely escalate into a broader war between the United States and China. That is, the war would be contained in the area around Taiwan; the main combatants would probably be limited to the United States, China, and Japan; and active hostilities would probably end after a relatively short time. Nonetheless, such a war would probably result in a bitter relationship between the United States and China, comparable in some ways to that between the United States and the Soviet Union during the Cold War. China might well accelerate the buildup of its military capabilities with an eye toward waging a second, this time successful, campaign to claim Taiwan. This military competition would likely also be accompanied by a broader deterioration in Sino-U.S. relations, with mutual trade and investment falling dramatically or even ceasing, and each country demanding that its allies not cooperate with its rival. Countries in Asia might find themselves under pressure to choose between good relations with the United States and good relations with China.

---

[10] This case includes situations in which Taiwan formally declares independence and is recognized as an independent country by the United States and other countries, so long as Beijing refuses to accept Taiwan's independence.

Nonetheless, even under these circumstances, the relationship between the United States and China after an inconclusive war over Taiwan would have important differences from the one between the United States and the Soviet Union during the Cold War. Unlike the Soviet Union, China is closely integrated into the world economy. With the exception of Japan, most countries in Asia would likely regard the importance of maintaining good relations with Beijing as outweighing any concerns about China having used force against Taiwan. They would resist U.S. pressure to choose between Washington and Beijing, preferring to maintain good relations with both. This logic would apply even more strongly to countries outside the region, which would be even less concerned about China's use of force.

For its part, because China's economic development—and the growing military strength that has resulted from it—has been so dependent on external trade and investment, Beijing would have strong reasons to maintain good relations with the rest of the world. Thus, assuming that active hostilities over Taiwan ended relatively quickly, it seems likely that, outside of the United States, Taiwan, and Japan, much of the world would soon resume trading with and investing in China. Exports to the United States, Taiwan, and Japan, however, represent about 40 percent of China's export earnings and about 15 percent of China's gross domestic product. Similarly, investment from the United States, Taiwan, and Japan represents at least 20 percent of foreign direct investment in China.[11] These high percentages of trade and investment mean that warring with, and thereby cutting off economic relations with, the United States, Taiwan, and Japan would cause China's economy to shrink by about 15 percent in the near term, even if the rest of the world continued to trade with and invest in China.

---

[11] National Bureau of Statistics of China (2005), pp. 51, 631–634, 644–646. Percentages are based on 2004 trade and investment statistics. Exports to the United States, Taiwan, and Japan as a percentage of China's total exports were estimated under the assumption that most of China's exports to Hong Kong are subsequently re-exported to other countries. Investment from the United States, Japan, and especially Taiwan is probably higher than estimated, since about 14 percent of China's direct foreign investment appears to originate from the Virgin and Cayman islands. Much of this is probably Taiwanese money successfully evading Taipei's restrictions on investment in mainland China.

This would push the country into a major recession. Moreover, since China's economic growth has been driven largely by foreign trade and investment, subsequent economic recovery and growth would be significantly slowed by the absence of trade and investment from the three countries.

Damage this severe to China's economy would threaten the Chinese government's hold on power, possibly forcing the replacement of the responsible individuals with others—or even replacement of the entire form of government. It is possible that a new government could be much more accommodating on the Taiwan issue, in which case U.S.-China relations might be quickly repaired, as we discuss in the next subsection. But the new government could instead be much more stridently nationalist and anti-Western, converting a conflict over Taiwan into a true cold war, pitting the United States and its allies against China and its allies (if any). In this situation, the region would be divided between the group of countries aligned with China and the group aligned with the United States. Such a cold war could stymie political and economic evolution in East and Southeast Asia, put extreme pressure on the U.S. military posture both in East Asia and globally, and deal a disastrous setback to China's efforts to build a modern, prosperous society.[12]

If the Chinese leadership survived the economic crisis that would follow a war over Taiwan, however, or if a successor regime placed a similar priority on export-led economic growth while refusing to accept Taiwan's independence, China would undoubtedly eventually recover from the effects of a cutoff of economic relations with the United States, Taiwan, and Japan. Foreign trade and investment patterns would adjust to make up, at least partially, for the lack of participation from these countries in China's economy, and China would probably resume solid, if less rapid, economic growth.

---

[12] Another possibility would be a China with a divided or ineffective central government, in which case China would offer little direct threat to the United States but also would not be capable of making commitments regarding Taiwan that would necessarily be binding over the long term.

The direct and indirect effects of a war with mainland China would likely damage Taiwan's economy badly.[13] The effects on the economies of the United States and Japan would be less significant. U.S. exports to China, for example, represent about 5 percent of total U.S. export earnings and less than 0.5 percent of the U.S. gross domestic product.[14] Although a war with China and the associated cutoff of economic relations would undoubtedly affect the U.S. economy, it would quickly recover, and the long-term economic effects would be manageable.

Violent Independence with U.S. Intervention

If China used force against Taiwan, the United States intervened, and China was defeated, it is possible that Beijing might accept Taiwan's independence. Under these circumstances, the subsequent relationship between the United States and China would undoubtedly be mutually suspicious. However, a Chinese government—which would not necessarily be the same as the one that had initiated the conflict—that recognized Taiwan as an independent country would of necessity be fundamentally pragmatic and willing to take whatever measures were needed to advance the material interests of the nation. Given that China possesses nuclear weapons capable of reaching the continental United States, the United States would have no way of forcing surrender terms on Beijing. Thus, even a badly defeated China would have no reason to accept Taiwan's independence *except* to restore good relations with the United States. Beijing's renunciation of its claim to Taiwan would eliminate China's primary military threat to U.S. interests, so in this situation, the United States would have little reason to withhold cooperation with China and a strong incentive to reward it for taking this step. In many ways, the U.S.-China relationship in this situation would probably look much the way it does today, with each country continuing to behave in ways that the other finds at least intermit-

---

[13] Aside from the direct effects, exports to the mainland now represent about 30 percent of Taiwan's export earnings and more than 15 percent of Taiwan's gross domestic product. See National Bureau of Statistics, (2005), p. 631; Council for Economic Planning and Development (2004), pp. 15, 203. Percentages are as of 2003.

[14] National Bureau of Statistics (2005), p. 634; U.S. Census Bureau (2006), "Income, Expenditures, & Wealth: Gross Domestic Product and Gross State Product" (2006).

tently objectionable, but engaging in a robust economic relationship and cooperating in a number of areas. Resolving the Taiwan issue, however, would significantly reduce prospects for a direct conflict and the fundamental tensions between the two.[15]

Violent Unification Despite U.S. Intervention

At the other extreme, it is possible that China could succeed in achieving unification through force even if the United States came to Taiwan's defense.[16] Although such an outcome may appear improbable at present, its possibility will increase as China's military capabilities grow relative to those of Taiwan and the United States.

A defeat in an attempted U.S. defense of Taiwan would be a watershed in contemporary security affairs, marking the end of U.S. military dominance in Asia. Like China in the violent irresolution and violent independence cases described in the previous sections, Washington would have the choice of accepting the outcome or of seeing it as the initial battle in a more prolonged Sino-U.S. war that, once again, could share some features with the Cold War and with the deleterious consequences described previously, under "Violent Irresolution with U.S. Intervention." Because of the damage to U.S. stature and influence in the world, however, the U.S. reaction would likely be much more severe than in that earlier case.

Conflict Without U.S. Intervention

The preceding three scenarios all assumed that the United States intervened on behalf of Taiwan. It is possible, however, that, for whatever

---

[15] It is also possible, however, that such a Chinese government would be unstable and transitory, similar to that of Weimar Germany, and that it would be replaced by a regime that did not accept Taiwan's independence. In this case, the situation would revert to the "violent irresolution" described in the previous section.

[16] China has stated that its "One Country, Two Systems" model is conditional on peaceful unification. So, in this scenario, the model would not necessarily be implemented. In fact, an invasion of Taiwan would likely require deployment of both mainland military forces and administrative officials, which the model does not allow.

reason, the United States would choose not to intervene.[17] In this case, three alternative outcomes are again possible.

Violent Unification Without U.S. Intervention

It is possible to imagine almost any type of Chinese polity—from a mature democracy to an expansionist dictatorship—using force against Taiwan. If the United States chose not to intervene and if the use of force succeeded, the consequences for U.S.-China relations would be strongly conditioned by the reasons underlying Washington's decision not to intervene.[18]

If the U.S. decision not to assist in Taiwan's defense was driven by the perception that Taiwan had unreasonably provoked Beijing or if it followed some other rupture in U.S.-Taiwan relations, China's actions might be viewed as unwelcome but understandable (or even inevitable) and might not cause a fundamental alteration of U.S.-China relations. This would be one of the few cases in which subsequent Sino-U.S. relations would largely depend on factors unrelated to how Taiwan's status was resolved.

If, however, China's action were to be seen as exploiting a window of U.S. weakness or preoccupation elsewhere, or if the U.S. decision not to intervene was highly controversial in the United States, the consequences for U.S.-China relations could be profoundly negative. A United States that was forced by its own lack of options to stand by and watch as China "swallowed" Taiwan could be motivated to strive to undo the deed or at least to rebuild its security position in Asia to ensure that Beijing could never again expect to opportunistically gain from U.S. weakness. A cold war between Washington and Beijing, such as that described above under "Violent Irresolution with U.S. Intervention," might be the best outcome that could be expected

---

[17] Possible reasons include a perception that Taiwan had provoked the conflict, an inability to respond due to a crisis in the United States or elsewhere in the world, or a change in U.S. domestic politics or foreign policy calculus that resulted in a withdrawal of the U.S. security commitment to Taiwan.

[18] This situation includes cases in which China achieves unification through intimidation— that is, by threatening Taiwan with military violence without actually needing to take such action.

from such a course of events. Similarly, if the U.S. decision not to intervene provoked subsequent accusations about "Who lost Taiwan?" similar to the "Who lost China?" controversy that followed the Chinese Communists' victory in 1949, it could provoke a backlash that would cause U.S.-China relations to deteriorate to a point comparable to those described earlier, under "Violent Unification Despite U.S. Intervention."[19]

Violent Irresolution Without U.S. Intervention

The effects on U.S.-China relations of a failed Chinese attempt to conquer or coerce Taiwan when the United States did not intervene could vary widely. It is unlikely that any Chinese regime that seriously attempted to use force against Taiwan and failed would long survive, especially without being able to blame its failure on the intervention of an external power. However, it is difficult to predict what type of regime its replacement would be. The successor regime could be similar to its predecessor, with the principal difference being only the specific individual leaders involved. Alternatively, it could move China toward democracy, or it could be even more nationalistic, more deeply committed to regaining Taiwan whatever the costs. Thus, a failed attempt to take Taiwan using force could well profoundly affect U.S.-China relations by bringing to power a fundamentally new type of regime in China, but the consequences for the relationship would be highly unpredictable.

Violent Independence Without U.S. Intervention

Even more than in the Violent Independence with U.S. Intervention case, a scenario in which China attacked Taiwan, was defeated despite U.S. nonintervention, and subsequently formally recognized Taiwan as an independent country, is one in which the post-conflict government in Beijing—again, not necessarily the same or even of the same ilk as the one that initiated the failed war—would of necessity be fundamentally pragmatic. Such a government would likely be able to come to

---

[19] The authors are grateful to Richard Bush of the Brookings Institution for this observation.

terms with other realities of the international system and would focus on advancing China's strategic and material interests instead of undoing perceived wrongs of the past. Especially if the regime were replaced by a new one that Washington held relatively blameless for the attack on Taiwan, relations between the United States and China would likely improve in the wake of such a conflict.

CHAPTER THREE

Observations

Tables 3.1 and 3.2 lay out the cases discussed above and their basic implications for subsequent U.S.-China relations. Table 3.1 shows the nonviolent cases; Table 3.2 shows the trajectories involving Chinese use of force. As can be seen, although there are ten primary ways in which Taiwan's status could be resolved, there are only about five distinctly different outcomes for Sino-U.S. relations:

- a continuation of the current situation of strong economic ties and some diplomatic cooperation, but also a possibility of war
- a relationship that is essentially cooperative in all areas because Taiwan has voluntarily accepted unification with mainland China (which most likely has evolved into a democracy)
- a relationship in which the United States and China remain wary of each other but maintain strong economic ties and in which there is little chance of war
- a hostile relationship in which the United States and China have broken off economic ties with each other and their military forces confront each other across the Taiwan Strait
- a true cold war in which not only have the United States and China broken off economic ties and their military forces confront each other across the Taiwan Strait, but the United States exerts pressure on its allies in Asia and Europe to join Washington in ending economic and political cooperation with China.

This chapter returns to the question that initially motivated this exploration: What will U.S.-China relations be like after resolution of

Table 3.1
Nonviolent Trajectories for Cross-Strait Relations

Trajectory	Implications for U.S.-China Relations
Status quo	Strong economic ties Some diplomatic cooperation Continuing possibility of war
Peaceful unification	Little chance of war Strong economic ties Strong diplomatic cooperation
Peaceful independence	Little chance of war Strong economic ties Some diplomatic cooperation
Compromise resolution	Little chance of war Strong economic ties Some diplomatic cooperation

Table 3.2
Violent Trajectories for Cross-Strait Relations

Trajectory	Implications for U.S.-China Relations
U.S. intervenes; inconclusive war	Military standoff across Taiwan Strait Economic ties broken Little diplomatic cooperation
U.S. intervenes; forced unification	Hostile cold war United States attempts to isolate China
U.S. intervenes; violent independence	Little chance of subsequent war Strong economic ties Some diplomatic cooperation
No U.S. intervention; inconclusive war	Consequences for U.S.-China relations unpredictable
No U.S. intervention; forced unification	Consequences for U.S.-China relations unpredictable
No U.S. intervention; violent independence	Little chance of war Strong economic ties Some diplomatic cooperation

the Taiwan issue? Examining the seven cases in which Taiwan's status is actually resolved, it is clear that this depends very much on *how* it is resolved. Unsurprisingly, as Table 3.1 shows, almost any type of peaceful resolution implies that subsequent relations between the United States and China will be cooperative and peaceful. This is partly because the most significant possible trigger for conflict between the United States and China will have been removed but also because peaceful resolution of Taiwan's status implies a Chinese government that is pragmatic or pluralistic enough that either it is willing to accept something less than Taiwan's subordination to Beijing or at least that the people of Taiwan no longer feel threatened by this subordination.

If the issue is resolved violently, the implications for U.S.-China relations are more varied, with much depending on the specific nature of that resolution. If the result is forced unification for Taiwan, subsequent U.S.-China relations will most likely be those of a hostile cold war.[1] If an attempt to bring about unification through military force instead resulted in Beijing accepting formal independence for Taiwan, on the other hand, subsequent U.S.-China relations would almost certainly be cooperative and peaceful. Again, this would be not only because the most significant possible trigger for conflict between the United States and China would have been removed but also because a Chinese government that is pragmatic and flexible enough to recognize Taiwan's independence formally (which would quite likely be a different government from the one that started the war) would almost certainly be one that sought good relations with the United States as well.

To summarize the major findings of the analysis presented in this monograph, therefore, U.S.-China relations after the resolution of Taiwan's status could fall anywhere from close cooperation between two mature democracies to a Cold War–like confrontation. Unsurprisingly,

---

[1] If this forced unification occurred despite U.S. military intervention, the result would almost certainly be a hostile cold war. If forced unification occurred in the context of a U.S. decision not to intervene, however, there are two possibilities. One is a hostile cold war; the other is that U.S.-China relations could continue in their current state of wariness but not outright hostility. Which of these occurred would depend on the reasons behind Washington's abstention.

if the resolution of Taiwan's status is peaceful, relations will almost certainly be cooperative, regardless of the specific nature of that resolution. Less obviously, if the result of a violent attempt to resolve Taiwan's status is formal independence for the island, subsequent U.S.-China relations would likely also be cooperative because only a fundamentally pragmatic Chinese regime would be willing to recognize Taiwan as an independent country. If the result is forcible unification for Taiwan, however, the United States and China will most likely find themselves in a hostile cold war.

Perhaps even more fundamental than the observation that how the Taiwan issue is resolved will dramatically affect the nature of subsequent U.S.-China relations is the recognition that both how the Taiwan issue is resolved and the nature of subsequent U.S.-China relations will largely be determined by the orientation of China's government. A pragmatic, self-confident Chinese government is both more likely to be able to come to some sort of peaceful accommodation with Taiwan and more likely to have amicable relations with the United States. An inflexible, nationalistic Chinese government, on the other hand, is both less apt to be able to resolve the Taiwan issue and likely to have an adversarial relationship with the United States.

For more than 25 years, U.S. policy has, above all else, sought to ensure that any resolution of Taiwan's status occurs peacefully. The analysis here suggests that this has indeed been the correct policy, as the consequences of a peaceful resolution of Taiwan's status are almost uniformly positive for the United States. The analysis here also shows, however, that the consequences of violent unification are almost certainly negative. Thus, as China's power and confidence in its military capabilities grow, it is important for the United States to maintain the capability to deter and, if necessary, defeat an attempt by Beijing to achieve unification through force.

Bibliography

Brown, Michael E., Sean M. Lynn-Jones, and Steven E. Miller, eds., *Debating the Democratic Peace*, Cambridge, Mass.: Massachusetts Institute of Technology Press, 1997.

Bush, Richard, Brookings Institution, personal communication with authors, Washington, D.C., June, 2006

Cliff, Roger, "China's Peaceful Unification Strategy," *The American Asian Review*, Vol. XIII, No. 4, Winter 1996.

Council for Economic Planning and Development, Republic of China, *Taiwan Statistical Data Book*, Taipei, Taiwan, 2004.

Farber, Henry S., and Joanne Gowa, "Polities and Peace," *International Security*, Vol. XX, No. 2, Fall 1995, pp. 123–146.

Mainland Affairs Council, Executive Yuan, Republic of China, "Unification or Independence?" statistical chart from poll on Public Opinion on Cross-Strait Relations in the Republic of China, Taipei, Taiwan, 2006. As of January 9, 2007: http://www.mac.gov.tw/english/english/pos/p9007e.htm

Mansfield, Edward D., and Jack Snyder, *Electing to Fight: Why Emerging Democracies Go to War*, Cambridge, Mass.: MIT Press, 2005.

National Bureau of Statistics of China, *China Statistical Yearbook*, Beijing: China Statistics Press, 2005.

Robertson, Benjamin, and Melinda Liu, "Can the Sage Save China?" *Newsweek International*, March 20, 2006.

Spiro, David E., "The Insignificance of the Liberal Peace," *International Security*, Vol. IXX, No. 2, Fall 1994, pp. 50–86.

U.S. Census Bureau, "Foreign Commerce & Aid: Exports and Imports," *Statistical Abstract of the United States*, 2006. As of September 11, 2006: http://www.census.gov/compendia/statab/foreign_commerce_aid/exports_and_imports/

U.S. Census Bureau, "Income, Expenditures, & Wealth: Gross Domestic Product and Gross State Product," *Statistical Abstract of the United States*, 2006. As of September 11, 2006:
http://www.census.gov/compendia/statab/income_expenditures_wealth/gross_domestic_product_and_gross_state_product/

Made in the USA
Middletown, DE
12 March 2023